# Fluidity

A woman's life hidden in words

Dorie Snow

BookLeaf
Publishing

India | USA | UK

# Dedication

To the child inside of me I failed to protect, go now and live your life in color, whatever colors they may be.

# Preface

Life is not kind. That does not mean we have to be ruthless. Regardless of these things I still hold love in my heart and hope in my soul. Never give in to the fear, do not let it decide your fate. Nothing can dictate the expanse of your soul or the color of your light. Live your life in color, whatever colors they may be.

# Acknowledgements

My dearest Momma, Betty Ann, my babies all grown now, my soul companion Cassie who did not let me give up. To every professor who encouraged me to keep going despite the difficulties.

# 1. Magical Thinking

As the magic goes,
so shall I.
Marching along
and opposed so shall I.
Following the winter
bless my heart
deeply remiss
breathe in the
essence of spring.
My soul light to bring.
Start with a dream
and end with a kiss.

# 2. Crossroad

I find myself at a crossroad
The loneliness seeps
into my wakefulness
As if my breath
could not function
Without the silence
of an uttered word.
My heart vibrates
the echoes of betrayal
Therefore my isolation
will persist.

# 3. The Let Go

Morning light broke through the fog,
a coastal path, a climb, a dialogue.
The sky, once veiled, began to clear,
the ocean calm, no storms near.

No crashing waves, no pounding roar,
just fluid silence, a tranquil shore.
He thought the scene, so vast, so still,
might soften words, might bend their will.

They'd hiked this trail through passing years,
shared laughter, silence, joys, and fears.
But now, atop the rocky height,
he spoke his truth, her tears took flight.

No interruptions, just quiet cries,
her heart laid bare beneath the skies.
He faced her, knowing the walk back down
would carry weight, a heavy crown.

"We're unsuitable," he gently said,
"Incompatible." The words hung, spread.
A tinge of guilt, yet more relief,
no more pretense, no more grief.

He looked at her with softened eyes,
unaware of her internal cries.
Two selves at war, a silent fight,
one seeking day, one seeking night.

"Sometimes," he said, "you must release,
let go of one to find your peace.
Let me go." His voice, a plea,
a quiet end to what used to be.

Her eyes pressed shut, tears traced her face,
no words remained, no need to chase.
"Perhaps it's best," she softly sighed,
while in her mind, a darker tide.

"Perhaps my breath should be let go,"
her thoughts whispered, soft and low.
She opened eyes, drew one deep breath,
then turned away, embraced her death.

Step by step, a melody,
each footfall sang her elegy.

She turned to him, a fragile smile,
stretched out her arms, and paused awhile.

Then pushed herself off the cliff's edge,
no scream, no word, no final pledge.
She simply fell, she simply flew,
she simply let go—of him, of you.

He stood in shock, his freedom gained,
her freedom found, her pain unchained.
He'd asked her once to let him go,
and so she did—with breath laid low.

# 4. No Love for Me

There is no love for me
No support
No helpmate
No fairytale
Endless days of weary toil
Regrets and pain
Looking back
I wish to escape the lie
So many mistakes
So many misdirections
So much misunderstandings
I believed you to be sincere,
I believed you to be honest,
I believed you to be kind.
No one stays
No one stays true
No one stays loyal
No one means what they say
Always an angle
Always a game

Always a manipulation
I give and give
They take and take
Leaving you an empty vessel
Struggling to feed
Not only my body, but the
Heart and soul they
shattered

# 5. Lily

I was born a lily
in a garden of roses.
I grew up like a rose,
my frame of reference
strength and resilience.
I dreamed of being a rose,
my petals glistening,
my stem, strong
thorny and protective.
I dreamed of radiating essence,
spreading my leaves.
I wanted nothing more
than to be the bouquet
that was given for love,
life, laughter, and happiness.
But I was born a lily,
and even though my mind,
my dreams,
my inspirations were for love,
my bouquet is only given

to express the sorrow
of passing.
I am beautiful in my own way,
I am delicate and fragile
like the circle of life.
I rejected my reality
for so very long
but in the end, I was still giving away
in the presence of mourning.

# 6. Marriage

Thank you for the reminders.
I need them to be able
to improve myself.
Monitor the schedule.
Make the list.
My smile is fake.
I flinch when
he walks
into the room.
I hide in my garden,
my parent volunteer groups,
my church.
My kitchen.
If I hide,
I will be safe for
only a moment.
If I am perfect,
then I won't be hurt,
hit in front
of the children.

A lady doesn't complain.
She does her duty
for her husband and family.
Even when it hurts,
smile
and say thank you.
I only rest
when he snores
and then I can sleep.
But I don't sleep.
I plan how to make
the next day perfect.

# 7. Memories of My Mother

I remember the smell of clean.
The cold hands touching my face.
Perfume.
Sheer curtains blowing in the breeze
from the window above the bed.
She had a scarf on her head, covering her hair.
The sheets were cool, crisp, clean and inviting.
There was so much sunlight.
Her face was haloed in the light.
My tummy hurts so she pats my back.
I felt safe and warm.
I felt comfort, even though she was crying.
Silent tears not sobs.
She sang *How Great Thou Art*
and her whole voice lulled me to sleep.
When I woke up,
I was grown.

# 8. Indoctrination

If the hours are the mirror to the soul,
cover them quickly
with an air of indifference.
The true opposite of love
is indifference.
Hate is the lover of rage,
neither are acceptable.
Hide, hide behind
the deep cold light.
Save your heart
from further slight.

# 9. Lily

I was born a lily
in a garden of roses.
I grew up like a rose,
my frame of reference
strength and resilience.
I dreamed of being a rose,
my petals glistening,
my stem, strong
thorny and protective.
I dreamed of radiating essence,
spreading my leaves.
I wanted nothing more
than to be the bouquet
that was given for love,
life, laughter, and happiness.
But I was born a lily,
and even though my mind,
my dreams,
my inspirations were for love,
my bouquet is only given

to express the sorrow
of passing.
I am beautiful in my own way,
I am delicate and fragile
like the circle of life.
I rejected my reality
for so very long
but in the end, I was still giving away
in the presence of mourning

# 10. The In-Between

Your opinion doesn't change the color of my reality.
Your indoctrination doesn't change my culture.
Your vitriol and division do not change my ethnicity.
No paper bag is a testament to my ancestral roots.
No percentage changes my status on the census.
Is not my color a representation of violence?
My privilege changes with the tones of politics.
I'm only allowed in spaces when it's convenient.
When I can be a token nod for a data point.
Sometimes I'm accepted into their spaces, but I grew
up in yours.
I talked different, I looked different,
I can pass only minimally.
My soul burns with the pain of my ancestors.
My heart bleeds for every lost person
to our collective systematic destruction.
I advocate and I'm turned away.
I fight and I am shamed.
I follow our traditions as I was raised to do and I am
called an appropriator.

I can't change the color of my skin just like you can't
change yours.
Where is my space to grow and thrive when I
am rejected by both of my communities?
I live in the grey area of acceptance.
I live in the in between.

# 11. Mediator

Bring the peace
harmonize quiet.
the scorching flow
of bitter turbulence,
inside.
Drown the sorrow
with empathy
quiet the mind.
Tell yourself the story
keep the love inside.
Sleep, sleep, sleep,
quiet the mind.

# 12. Departures

Walk-through fear
departure from dependence of safety.
Apathy is safe,
pain is safe, disassociate.
A normal feeling, an old bathrobe shrouding your
nakedness.
What is the fear, pain is so normal?
What is the walk?
When alone is the normal.
What is the departure when apathy?
numb void is the safety?
Why leave when the hurt is inside?
Why add more hurt from the outside?
How do you depart from the fear
of not having the safety of oblivion?

# 13. Pear

If I offer you a pear,
I am offering you, my silence.
If I suggest you taste
the sweet tinged
with bitterness at the core,
I am turning my back
on your progression.
If I take time to
slice the pear,
and present it beautifully,
I am struggling
with my decision
to let you go.
As I carefully
arrange the pieces
on a plate,
To look like a flower
I will hand it to you
With sadness and gratitude

As I gently ask you
To leave my life.

# 14. Hopeless

I feel small in my skin.
My physical presence is diminished
by the enormity of my tortured thoughts.
I feel as if I cower and hide in the shadows
so that no one can find me.
I feel lost in the ether of my mind,
muffled voices, bleeding,
shadows of different times,
places and people.

# 15. Masking

Shut down,
shut off, not allowed the feelings in.
If I go past the rage, the anger,
then I will cease to be.
The betrayal of your actions,
regardless of your words,
rips a hole inside of my heart,
so wide, and deep there is nothing left to sustain its
function for you,
only rage.

# 16. Garden

Craft, keep the good,
the shadow does not steal the joy.
Every seed of joy needs a place to take root
flourish.
There is nothing better to heal the soul
than the fresh green of plants,
rich and fragrance soil with a breath of sunlight.
If we are to bring the shadow to light,
we must find the land beyond the boundaries,
The keepers of the house,
we can go away and come back
then see our place with new eyes and brilliant color

# 17. Tulip

She wanders out to a little patch
Of flowers blooming
Her golden pigtails bouncing
With her happy rhythm.
The winter is over
Spring is just arriving
She's looking for Hope
In the barren straw like appearance
of the garden floor.
She squats down
In her little pink dress
Looking closely for any sign
of hope.
She notices the little green sprouts
smiles broadly
She knows her mommy has not left her
Because the tulips were coming alive.

# 18. Rose

Why must you perfect me?
Am I not already strong enough?
Do not protect my bloom?
Are my roots, not steady?
My thorns not aggressive?
When you look at me
You see a possession
Something you must own
Something you must tame
You manipulate me
To strive harder
Forever perfection
That is your perception
I cannot achieve
I reach and I reach
I grind and I work
I must be better
But still, you prune
Still, you cut
Still, you change my balance

Still, you bring me down
And when I blossom
Radiantly beautiful
Profoundly intelligent
Astonishingly capable
You cut me down
Place me in a vase
To stare at me
Until I wither
Broken, beat down
A discarded possession.

# 19. Gentleness

Today I was most gentle.
No excessive accessories
My hair carefully and crafted into a mess.
I spoke softly yet earnestly.
I felt the awakening of a mother goddess,
inside of me.
I smiled gently,
looking into his unburdened eyes,
And spoke quietly.

# 20. Longing

My heart is full of longing
Like the ocean breeze caresses my skin
Tumbles my hair
I dream of your touch
I miss you most
In the early dawn
When wakefulness releases
Me from dreaming

# 21. Destiny

Mountain
Mist-shrouded landscape
Dark clouds hang over the truth
The wind blows the seeds
Nature mourns the passing season
Time flows through the river
Leaves move downstream
Never met, but in a moment

www.ingramcontent.com/pod-product-compliance
Lightning Source LLC
Chambersburg PA
CBHW071236140726
47996CB00007B/2625